Who Was
Leonardo da Vinci?

Who Was Leonardo da Vinci?

by Roberta Edwards

illustrated by True Kelley

Penguin Workshop

For Tanni Tytel—RE
For Eloise and Charlotte Lindblom—TK

PENGUIN WORKSHOP
An Imprint of Penguin Random House LLC, New York

If you purchased this book without a cover, you should be aware that this book is stolen property. It was reported as "unsold and destroyed" to the publisher, and neither the author nor the publisher has received any payment for this "stripped book."

Visit us online at www.penguinrandomhouse.com.

Library of Congress Control Number: 2005014639

ISBN 9780448443010

Contents

Who Was
Leonardo da Vinci?

Some people are enormously talented . . . and then there is Leonardo da Vinci. He lived at a time when there were many extremely talented people all around him. Even so, he stood out.

He could draw and paint better than anyone. One of his paintings, the *Mona Lisa,* is the most famous painting in the world. He was a scientist hoping to unlock the secrets of the natural world. He was an engineer and inventor. He designed a bicycle that would have worked—three hundred years before the first bike was actually built.

Leonardo's lira da braccia

He was an excellent athlete. A fine musician. *And* he was handsome. (Although there are no known paintings of him, whenever people of the day described him, they always mentioned his good looks.)

"I want to work miracles," he stated. Yet he often met with failure. And while he could be charming, he mistrusted almost everyone. He was a loner. He had no family of his own. For sixteen years, he didn't even have a home of his own.

By his own standards, Leonardo was a disappointment. He never reached the goals he set for himself. His greatest works were left unfinished. Nevertheless, what he did achieve in sixty-seven years still sets the standard for human excellence. It is hard to imagine someone doing better.

Chapter 1
An Unwanted Boy

On April 15, 1452, in a tiny hill town in Italy, a baby boy was born. His father was a well-to-do businessman, Ser Piero. His mother, Caterina, was a poor young peasant girl. We don't even know her last name. Their baby was named Leonardo. Because the town he came from was called Vinci, he was known as Leonardo da Vinci. That means

Leonardo from
Vinci.

Leonardo's parents weren't
married. His father was ashamed
of the baby and left him with his
mother. Ser Piero married another
woman, someone more respectable, and
started a new family. He moved nearby
to the busy city of Florence. Caterina
did not want to keep her baby, either. She cared
for him for only a year or two. Then she, too,
married someone else and began a new family.

So what was to become of little Leonardo?

Ser Piero's answer was to leave the baby with his
parents. But Leonardo's grandparents were old—
his grandfather was eighty-five at the time. At their
age, what did they want with a toddler? Still, they
took him in. They fed him, clothed him, and gave
him a home. But little else. No one loved the little

boy. The only person who showed interest in him was an uncle named Francesco.

Francesco was a farmer and he loved the beautiful countryside around Vinci. He would take long walks in the hills, which were covered with olive trees.

Leonardo would go with him. It was there on these walks that Leonardo grew to love the natural world. The rolling shapes of the hills. The silvery leaves of the olive trees. The flight of birds. And the soft misty sunlight.

Everywhere he went, Leonardo took a little notebook with him. He made drawings of anything that interested him. A plant. Ducks in a stream. Flowers. An insect. Some cows. Paper was very

valuable, but Leonardo was lucky. Because of his father's business, there was always a supply. It was one of the most important things Ser Piero ever gave his son.

PARCHMENT AND PAPER

PARCHMENT IS MADE FROM THE SKINS OF
ANIMALS SUCH AS SHEEP, CALVES, OR
GOATS. THE SKIN IS DRIED AND TREATED
UNTIL IT BECOMES FLAT AND PAPERLIKE.

PARCHMENT IS MUCH STRONGER THAN
PAPER. IT IS MORE EXPENSIVE, TOO. THE
BEAUTIFUL PRAYER BOOKS AND BIBLES
COPIED BY HAND IN THE MIDDLE AGES
WERE ON PARCHMENT. PARCHMENT IS
RARELY USED TODAY.

PAPER WAS FIRST MADE IN CHINA
ALMOST TWO THOUSAND YEARS AGO
BY USING BARK FROM THE MULBERRY
TREE. (TODAY, THE FINEST PAPER IS
MADE FROM
CLOTH RAGS.)
PAPER WAS MADE
BY WETTING
AND POUNDING
THE MATERIAL UNTIL
IT SEPARATED INTO
FIBERS OR STRANDS.
THESE WERE THEN BROKEN
DOWN INTO A LIQUIDLIKE
SUBSTANCE THAT WAS
POURED ONTO A MESH MOLD. AFTER
THE SUBSTANCE DRAINED ON THE
MOLD, IT COULD BE LIFTED OFF AS A
SHEET OF PAPER. IN EUROPE, PAPER
WAS INTRODUCED BY THE MOORS
OF NORTHERN AFRICA. THE FIRST
PAPERMAKING MILL WAS BUILT IN SPAIN
AROUND 1150.

Mulberry Tree

Even when he was a young boy, Leonardo had an amazing talent for drawing. Drawings seemed to flow out of his fingers onto the paper. His rabbits and birds didn't look like drawings. They looked *alive*.

He understood the beauty of nature. He also knew its dangers. When he was only four years old, a terrible hurricane struck the countryside. Farms were destroyed, and many people were killed. Then when he was ten, the Arno River flooded Florence. Leonardo watched the storm and saw the flood; he never forgot either. All his life, he drew pictures of moving water.

Flooded Florence

Water was a source of life for animals and plants. It was also a source of destruction. Leonardo wanted to understand both sides of this force and to control its power.

His father must have been aware of his son's gift for drawing. All it would have taken was one look at one sketch. Ser Piero was a practical man. He knew Leonardo's choices in life were limited. Because Ser Piero never married Caterina, Leonardo could not attend a university. He could not be a lawyer and businessman like his father. He could not become a doctor. But he could work in one of the art studios in Florence. Being an artist was a respectable trade. Ser Piero decided to take Leonardo to the city. There, he arranged for him to live and work with a famous artist. His name was Andrea del Verrocchio. This was certainly the best thing Ser Piero ever did for his son. It changed Leonardo's life forever.

Verrocchio

Chapter 2
The Art Studio

Florence

During the 1400s, Florence was the most important, most exciting city in all the world. It was one of five city-states in what is now Italy. Being a city-state meant Florence had its own government. It was called the Signoria. But for many years the city was really ruled by one very rich, very powerful family called the Medici.

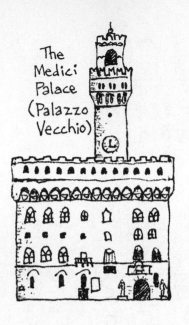

The Medici
Palace
(Palazzo
Vecchio)

The Medici men were art lovers. They built beautiful homes and churches and libraries in Florence. They wanted works of art to go inside all those buildings. Andrea del Verrocchio was one of the most famous artists working in Florence at the time. He had plenty of jobs. Leonardo was very lucky to study under such a master.

Leonardo was an apprentice. He was twelve at the time he went to Verrocchio's studio. All apprentices were boys. No girls were allowed. The apprentices were not paid. But they were given free room and food and a little money. At the studio they learned to become artists. For the first year, they had classes in drawing. After about seven or eight years they knew how to paint pictures,

create frescoes (paintings done directly onto walls), make statues out of marble or bronze, design pottery, silverware, objects of gold, and even design buildings.

Apprentices started at the bottom and worked their way up. They swept the studio, ran errands for the older artists, and cleaned up at the end of the day. There were no art supplies stores. So Leonardo and the other apprentices learned to make paintbrushes

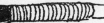

and paints. For the brushes, hairs from different animals were stuck into wooden handles. Hog bristles, for instance, made good, hard brushes. Squirrel fur was used for softer brushes. The artists painted with a kind of paint

mortar and pestle

Red: cochineal beetles

egg yolk

Yellow: buckthorn berries

Blue: lapis lazuli stone

called tempera. Its base was egg, not oil. (Painting with oil paints first started in the Netherlands; in Italy, artists did not start using oil paint until the 1470s.) Leonardo was taught to make colors. Blue came from grinding a stone called lapis lazuli into dust. Red came from crushing tiny beetles. Yellow came from the juice of one kind of berry.

At that time, canvas was not used for paintings. An artist painted on a flat panel of wood instead. But the wood had to be prepared first. Boiling kept it from splitting or cracking later on. Then glue was brushed on. After that, a coat of fine plaster called gesso was put on. This gave the

panel a nice, smooth surface for painting. All these steps were jobs for the apprentices.

Verrocchio's studio was always busy.

RISING UP THE LADDER

VERROCCHIO'S STUDIO WAS TYPICAL OF ITS DAY. APPRENTICES WERE AT THE VERY BOTTOM OF THE LADDER. ABOVE THEM WERE WORKERS CALLED JOURNEYMEN. THEY HAD MANY YEARS' EXPERIENCE AND HELPED TEACH THE APPRENTICES. THEY WERE ABLE WORKERS BUT WERE NOT GOOD ENOUGH YET TO JOIN THE GUILD OF PAINTERS. LIKE A UNION, THE GUILD WAS A GROUP THAT PROTECTED THE INTERESTS OF ITS MEMBERS. THERE WERE GUILDS FOR MANY DIFFERENT PROFESSIONS SUCH AS LEATHER WORKERS, DRUGGISTS, AND WEAVERS. VERROCCHIO'S BEST ASSISTANTS WERE ALREADY MEMBERS OF THE ARTISTS' GUILD AND THUS WERE KNOWN AS MASTERS. AT THE VERY TOP OF THE STUDIO WAS VERROCCHIO HIMSELF: THE MASTER OF MASTERS.

Master of Masters

Masters

Assistants

↑ GUILD MEMBERS

Journeymen

Apprentices

SUBJECTS OF PAINTINGS

IN LEONARDO'S TIME, PATRONS ORDERED TWO KINDS OF PAINTINGS. THEY EITHER WANTED PORTRAITS, WHICH WERE PICTURES OF THEMSELVES OR FAMILY MEMBERS, OR THEY WANTED RELIGIOUS PAINTINGS, WHICH SHOWED MOMENTS FROM THE LIFE OF JESUS AND THE SAINTS. THERE WERE NO LANDSCAPE PAINTINGS WHERE NATURAL SCENERY— A MOUNTAIN RANGE OR A VIEW OF A LAKE—WAS THE SUBJECT. NOR WERE THERE STILL-LIFE PICTURES, WHICH ARE PAINTINGS OF OBJECTS LIKE A BOWL OF FRUIT, A BUNCH OF FLOWERS IN A VASE, OR A TABLE SET FOR DINNER. OFTEN THESE SORTS OF THINGS WOULD APPEAR IN RELIGIOUS PAINTINGS, BUT THEY WEREN'T THE MAIN FOCUS. IN THE 1520S A GERMAN ARTIST NAMED ALBRECHT ALTDORFER WAS THE FIRST TO DO LANDSCAPE PAINTINGS. STILL-LIFE PAINTINGS WERE FIRST CREATED IN THE NETHERLANDS IN THE 1650S.

Portrait

Madonna + Child

Landscape

Still Life

At any one time the master and his assistants would be working on many different projects. Whatever Verrocchio's customers ordered, they'd make. As head of the studio, Verrocchio ran the business and drew up the contracts. The contract said exactly what the job was to be (for example, a statue of a soldier on horseback), how long it would take to finish it, how much it would cost, and what materials would be used. (Marble was more expensive than wood. Using wafer-thin pieces of gold called "gold leaf" on a painting added to its cost.) And only Verrocchio, the master, signed the works of art.

Right away Verrocchio saw that young Leonardo had special talent. He was a natural. So soon after he learned the basics of the trade, Leonardo was allowed to do more important work.

Customers—or patrons, as they were called—

often gave religious paintings to one of the important churches in Florence. A painting might be of Mary and the baby Jesus in the manger with Joseph and the Wise Men and shepherds. Sometimes the patron would have his wife and himself put into the picture, too. They might appear at the sides, kneeling and praying. They were almost always smaller in size than the saints.

On Sundays, when people came to church, they saw the beautiful painting of Mary and her baby *and* the patron who had paid for it. It was a lovely gift to the church. It also showed how rich and important the patrons were.

Verrocchio received a commission to do a painting of the baptism of Jesus. In it, Jesus is standing in a rocky stream. Saint John pours water over his head. At the left in the painting are two angels. Verrocchio himself painted almost everything except one of the angels. The angel is staring at Jesus in a way that shows he understands the importance of what he is watching. His face is sweet and wise. Leonardo painted the angel, and he is so full of life that everything else in the painting looks stiff. Verrocchio realized Leonardo was a genius. He had talent like no one he had ever seen before. Verrocchio understood that even he himself was not as good as his young apprentice. The story is that after he saw Leonardo's angel,

Leonardo's angel

Verrocchio never took up a paintbrush again. He went on to do more statues and items of gold. But he never did another painting.

statue of David by Verrocchio c. 1473

Chapter 3
The Wider World

Leonardo stayed at Verrocchio's workshop a long time—thirteen years. He became a master and a member of the guild. But he didn't move out to start a studio of his own. Perhaps Verrocchio's studio felt like a home to Leonardo, a place where he belonged and was wanted. Verrocchio was a kind master, and the two were probably quite close.

Florence was also an exciting place to live. It was full of new ideas. It was also a city with books. Lots of books. Until the mid-1400s, there were no printed books. Every book was copied by hand. Sometimes beautiful pictures were painted on the pages. The result was a work of art in itself. But it took a long time to make a single book. Then,

Johannes Gutenberg

around 1450, in Germany, a man named Johannes Gutenberg made a discovery. He figured out how to build a printing press. It used letters made of pieces of steel. They could be moved around to create different words. An inked page of type could be printed onto paper many times. The Bible was considered the most important book. So the first title printed was a Bible.

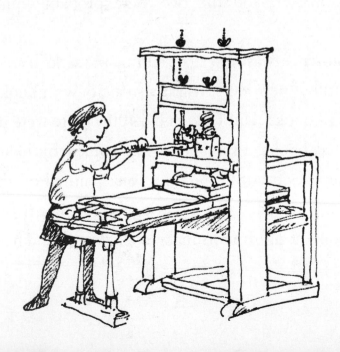

Very quickly, however, other books were printed as well. Books on math. Books of maps. Books by great thinkers of the past, like Plato and Aristotle. With more books available, more people started learning to read.

As a child, Leonardo had been taught to read and write. He also knew simple math. But that wasn't enough for him. He wanted to learn about everything. He couldn't attend a university. But he could teach himself. So he started buying and collecting books. He continued to do this all his life.

Artists needed math in order to make paintings look three-dimensional, or 3-D. In the Middle Ages, paintings didn't look realistic. The people in them looked flat, like a king or a queen on a playing card. The buildings looked flat, too, like pieces of scenery in a play. But in the 1400s an

A Middle Ages Painting by Duccio, Madonna and Child

artist named Filippo Brunelleschi figured out a way to make paintings appear to have depth. A person looking at a painting would be tricked

into thinking it was something in real space. For instance, figures close-up had to be much bigger than figures that were supposed to be far away. This is called painting in perspective. A painter needed math to measure out the correct spaces for figures on the wood panels.

Perspective

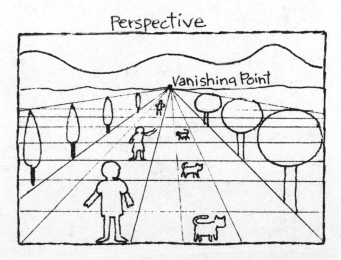

THE REBIRTH

THE FRENCH WORD *RENAISSANCE* MEANS "REBIRTH." IT IS THE NAME GIVEN TO ONE OF THE MOST EXCITING PERIODS IN HISTORY. IT'S IMPOSSIBLE TO GIVE EXACT DATES. BUT THE RENAISSANCE LASTED FROM THE EARLY OR MIDDLE 1400S TO AROUND 1600.

THE WORD IS FRENCH, BUT THE RED-HOT CENTER OF THE RENAISSANCE WAS ITALY. IT WAS A TIME OF CREATIVITY, NEW IDEAS, AND NEW WAYS OF THINKING. THE PURPOSE OF LIFE WAS NOT SOLELY TO DIE AND GO TO HEAVEN. THERE WERE GREAT THINGS THAT PEOPLE COULD ACCOMPLISH HERE ON EARTH. THE TERM "RENAISSANCE MAN" REFERS TO SOMEONE WHO IS GOOD AT EVERYTHING; LEONARDO WAS A CLASSIC EXAMPLE OF ONE. ARTISTS NOW CELEBRATED THE HUMAN BODY IN LIFELIKE PAINTINGS. SCHOLARS STUDIED WORKS OF ANCIENT GREEK AND ROMAN THINKERS THAT HAD BEEN LOST FOR CENTURIES. EXPLORERS SAILED TO UNKNOWN PARTS OF THE WORLD.

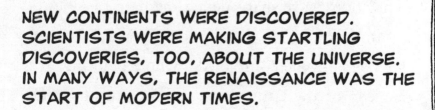

NEW CONTINENTS WERE DISCOVERED. SCIENTISTS WERE MAKING STARTLING DISCOVERIES, TOO, ABOUT THE UNIVERSE. IN MANY WAYS, THE RENAISSANCE WAS THE START OF MODERN TIMES.

Leonardo was a great painter because he followed the rules . . . and then made rules of his own. There was magic in his fingers. He blurred hills and valleys in the background of a painting. Just a little bit. They looked as if they were blending into the sky. This is exactly how faraway mountains appear to our eyes. They don't have sharp details or sharp outlines.

In 1478, when Leonardo was about twenty-six years old, he completed a whole painting. It is a scene of the Annunciation. The Annunciation was when an angel appeared to Mary. He told her that she was going to have a son named Jesus. In Leonardo's painting, Mary is wearing clothes that a woman of the time would have worn. She is sitting in a walled garden. The landscape in the background looks very much like the hills of Vinci. The picture is very peaceful, and yet it also has drama.

The *Annunciation* is one of only thirteen paintings that experts are sure that Leonardo painted. And three of those thirteen aren't finished.

The
Annunciation

Why did he paint so few? It wasn't that he died young. He lived well into his sixties. He wasn't lazy. He loved to work. For the *Annunciation*, he did dozens of drawings beforehand. Every curl of hair had to be right. Every blade of grass.

Perhaps Leonardo finished other paintings that may have gotten lost. Someday, in the future, a Leonardo painting may be found in a tiny church or a castle. That would be a great gift for the whole world.

But the fact is that Leonardo had trouble sticking with a project. If he got an order for a painting, the first steps interested him the most. He liked figuring out how to group the figures on the panel. That part was a challenge—like fitting together all the pieces of a puzzle. But finishing a painting, filling in the colors, wasn't as exciting. So very often he left his work undone. Also, his patrons could be fussy. And Leonardo did not like to be told what to do. He was a genius, after all!

By 1478, Florence was not the peaceful, pleasant
city it had been. The Medici family and another
powerful family were at war with each other. There
were plots to kill the Medici rulers. The streets
were dangerous.

At age thirty, Leonardo decided it was time for

a change. He left Florence to go north to Milan, another city-state. There, he hoped to work for the ruler of Milan, a scheming duke named Ludovico Sforza.

Chapter 4
Moving On

Duke Sforza

Milan had a famous university. But it was not a center for famous artists like Florence was. But Ludovico Sforza was very interested in the arts. The duke liked to give big parties. He like to put on pageants. He also wanted someone to design new weapons for him. (The city-states were often at war with one another.)

All of this interested Leonardo. He wrote a letter to the duke. In it, he listed everything he was good at. Some of it was bragging. He said he could design buildings and bridges, warships and huge cannons. Nobody knows if Leonardo ever sent the letter. There also is a story about a present that Leonardo gave the duke. The duke loved music. Leonardo did, too. So he made a lute. (This was like a violin, with strings and a bow.) It was made of silver—and was in the shape of a horse's skull! It had to be played upside down. Whether this is true or not, one thing is certain: The duke did eventually hire Leonardo.

ram's horns attached to horse's skull

decorated to look like a bird

So off Leonardo went to Milan. Whatever the duke wanted, Leonardo would create. He worked for the duke for many years, until the duke was forced from power.

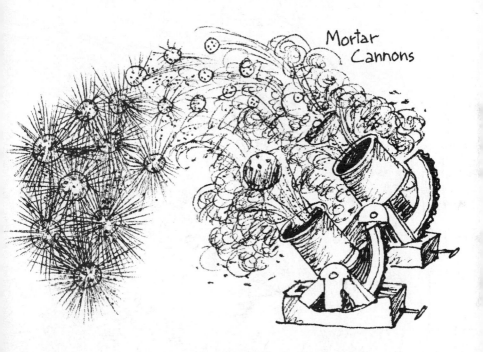

Mortar Cannons

When the duke's nephew was married, there was a huge feast. Leonardo was in charge of the party after the feast. He built incredible stage sets.

They were for a play known as *The Feast of Paradise*.
What a spectacle it must have been: A mountain
was split in two; inside it was a beautiful model of
the heavens. Actors in fancy costumes represented

the different planets. The twelve signs of the zodiac were lit by torches. Everything turned around and around.

THE UNIVERSE

IN THE SECOND CENTURY A.D., THERE
WAS A FAMOUS GREEK ASTRONOMER
NAMED PTOLOMY. HE BELIEVED THAT
THE EARTH WAS THE CENTER OF THE
UNIVERSE. THE OTHER PLANETS AND
THE SUN MOVED AROUND THE EARTH.
PEOPLE ACCEPTED THIS BELIEF UNTIL
THE MIDDLE OF THE 1500S. A POLISH
ASTRONOMER NAMED NICOLAUS
COPERNICUS SAID THE EARTH WAS
NOT THE CENTER OF THE UNIVERSE.
THE SUN DID NOT REVOLVE AROUND
IT. INSTEAD, THE EARTH—AND ALL THE
OTHER PLANETS—REVOLVED AROUND
THE SUN. HE WAS RIGHT. BUT IT TOOK
MANY YEARS BEFORE THIS FACT WAS
ACCEPTED.

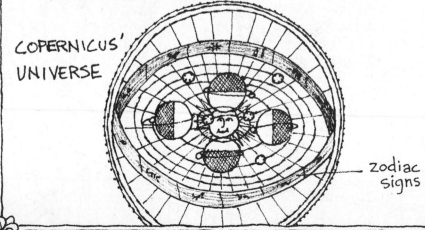

COPERNICUS'
UNIVERSE

zodiac
signs

Some of Leonardo's work was much more practical. He found a better way to heat the water for the duchess's bath. He also built a series of canals. Another project was something Leonardo worked on for years and was never able to finish; even at the end of his life, he was still dreaming about his "horse."

The duke wanted a giant statue of a horse. The statue was to honor the memory of his father. He didn't want it to just be big—he wanted it to be huge. The biggest ever. For years, Leonardo made sketches of how the horse statue might look. He studied the horses in the duke's stables. He made wax models. He even cut into the muscles and bones of dead horses. He wanted to know horses inside and out.

Leonardo's horse was to be more than three times the size of a real horse. Its front right leg would be lifted. It would be made of bronze. Eighty tons of metal were needed for a statue this big.

After ten years on the project, Leonardo finished a full-sized model of the horse in clay. It stood in the courtyard of the duke's castle. It was twenty-four feet high. Now everyone in Milan came to see what the statue would look like. And they all agreed: There had never been anything like it. But Leonardo still had much work ahead of

him. He made molds from clay for the different parts of the statue. After that, hot bronze would be poured into the molds. This was going to be a very tricky process, too. If the metal wasn't poured fast enough, it would crack as it grew hard. But Leonardo figured out how to avoid the cracking.

The duke collected all the metal that Leonardo needed. It really seemed as if the fabulous bronze statue would be made. But Leonardo never got to use the metal for his horse.

By 1494, the duke was afraid that soldiers from France were going to attack. What happened to all that bronze? The duke made it into cannons. Even so, the cannons did not stop the French. They took over Milan in 1499.

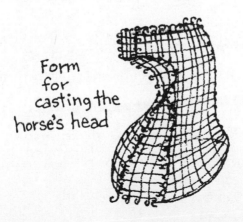

Form for casting the horse's head

And what happened to Leonardo's giant clay horse? The French used it for target practice. They shot arrows into it until it was completely destroyed. There was nothing left of all those long years of work. Leonardo's dream turned into dust.

It was not Leonardo's fault that the horse was never finished. However, another important job for the duke also came to an unhappy end. And this time, Leonardo was partly to blame.

Near the duke's castle was a monastery, a place where monks lived and prayed and studied. The duke planned to be buried there one day. He wanted Leonardo to paint a picture on one of the walls in the dining hall. This kind of painting is called a fresco. The most beautiful kind of fresco is also the hardest kind of painting to do. Water-based paint is put directly onto fresh plaster that hasn't dried. (In Italian, *fresco* means "fresh.") The artist must work quickly, and once the paint is brushed on, the artist can't go back and make changes.

The dining hall in the monastery was a very large room. It was big enough for fifty monks to eat in. Leonardo decided to choose a scene from the end of Jesus' life. He and his twelve followers are shown at a dinner table. This was a good choice for a painting in a dining hall. It is a very dramatic moment. Jesus tells his followers that one of them is going to betray him.

Leonardo made many drawings of ways to show thirteen figures seated at a table. He wandered through the streets of Milan looking for people to put in his fresco.

The fresco was to be painted on the wall so that it seemed to be part of the dining hall. It would be almost as if Jesus and his followers were in the same room with the monks. Even the table and the dishes in the painting were the same kind the monks used.

The fresco is called *The Last Supper* and is one of the most famous works of art in the world. Gentlemen from Milan would travel to the monastery to watch Leonardo paint. He didn't mind. In fact, he liked to hear their opinions of the picture.

A seventeen-year-old boy often came to watch, too. He grew up to be a writer and left accounts of *The Last Supper*. He wrote that sometimes Leonardo would come into the dining hall very early in the morning. He would paint the entire day from sunrise to sunset. He would not even stop to eat or drink anything. Then, on other days, he would stand in front of the painting and scold

himself. It wasn't good enough. And sometimes he would dash in from working on the horse statue. He would make one or two brushstrokes and then leave.

In the fresco, Jesus is shown in the center, with six men on either side of him. He looks very calm but sad. The followers react to his news with horror. Each side seems to back away from him, like a shock wave. One of the men, however, seems separated from the group. He is leaning forward, his arm on the table. He is named Judas. And he is the one who will betray Jesus.

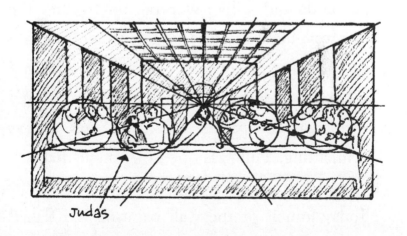

Judas

By 1497 *The Last Supper* was completed. It was so lifelike and so dramatic. All over Italy people talked about this beautiful, moving painting. Leonardo was known now as the greatest master of his day. Copies of *The Last Supper* were made by other artists. Engravings were made for people all over Europe to buy. Five hundred years later, it is still considered a work of genius.

So why isn't this a happy ending? It's because of damage to the painting. *The Last Supper* started to crack and peel less than fifty years after Leonardo finished it. It was Leonardo's fault.

Leonardo didn't like working on frescoes the regular way. He wanted to be able to go back and make changes. So instead, he tried something new. He put varnish on the wall and then painted it with tempera paints. Leonardo was always experimenting. This was one experiment that was a big mistake.

Today, much of the wall painting has flaked

off. Many of the faces are only half there. The colors are faded. Experts have tried to restore *The Last Supper*. They have made improvements. Still, there is a great deal of damage to this masterpiece. It is probably lucky that Leonardo can't see how it looks.

The duke was a good patron to Leonardo for many years. He kept Leonardo very busy. He also let him take jobs from other rich people in Milan.

It was in Milan that Leonardo took in a poor, ten-year-old boy. The year was 1490. The boy's name was Giacomo, but Leonardo called him Salai. That was a slang word meaning "rascal" or "demon." Salai was indeed a rascal. He lied. He broke things. He stole money from Leonardo and Leonardo's friends. In his notebooks, Leonardo wrote that Salai ate as much as two boys and made as much trouble as four.

Even so, Leonardo was very fond of Salai. He enjoyed spoiling him with presents. No matter how badly Salai behaved, Leonardo never asked him to leave. Salai stayed with him for the rest of Leonardo's life. Wherever Leonardo traveled, Salai went, too. He may have done chores for Leonardo. But he was much more important to him than a servant. Leonardo was not close to many people. He enjoyed being alone, free to think. He never had a family of his own. Perhaps Salai was the one person who was almost like family.

Chapter 5
Wandering

In 1499, when the French attacked, the duke lost his power. He fled Milan. Then, later on, he was captured. He died a prisoner in France.

In December of that year, Leonardo left Milan, too. Salai went with him. So did another old friend. Leonardo did not have a real home again for sixteen years. He took very little with him as he traveled from place to place. Only the most important things did he keep with him. Like his notebooks.

In Milan, he had started keeping notebooks full of drawings and ideas. Leonardo kept filling up notebooks for more than thirty years. His plan was to write an encyclopedia about everything.

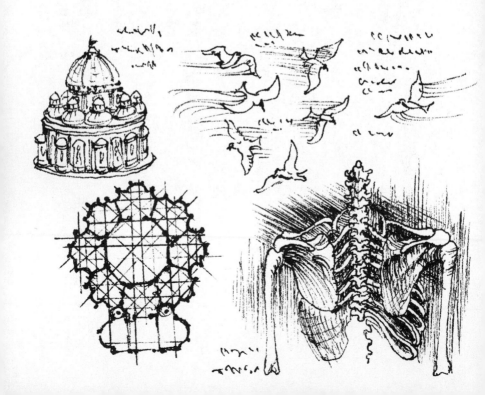

Like the horse statue, this was another great big project. And like the horse statue, it was a job he never completed. However, the notebooks are still priceless treasures. The pages are illustrated with beautiful drawings of everything that had interested Leonardo. They are among the most beautiful drawings in the world.

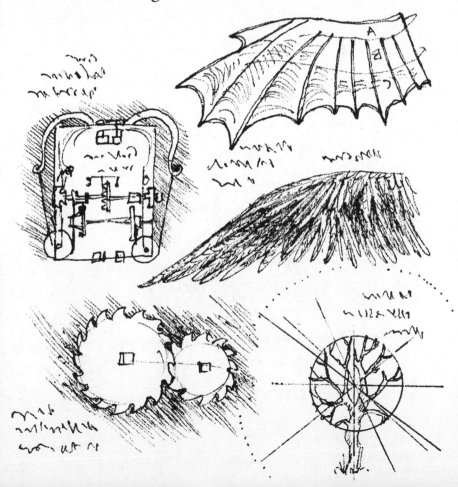

There probably were a total of about thirteen thousand notebook pages. But after his death, many pages were torn out and sold. Some notebooks were cut apart; some disappeared. Some were rediscovered hundreds of years later. Today, there are ten different collections of Leonardo's notebook pages. Only half the pages—about six thousand pages—are known to exist. They are in different places all over the world. There is always the hope that someday more notebook pages will turn up.

Life preserver

Bill Gates, the founder of Microsoft, bought one collection of pages. It is all about water. It is called Codex Atlanticus. Sometimes it is displayed in museums. In it are drawings of waves and currents, drawings of ripples in water, drawings of a drop of water as it splashes into a puddle. (Leonardo's eyes were so sharp, he could see all by himself what today's high-speed cameras can reveal.) There are experiments that Leonardo did with water.

Water shoes

Water-raising machine

Leonardo!

This is Mirror writing.

Can you read it?

A B C D E F G H I J K L M
N O P Q R S T U V W X Y Z

In all the notebooks, his handwriting is reversed. This is called mirror writing. A mirror must be held up to the writing before it reads correctly. Why did Leonardo write this way? Nobody knows. He was left-handed. So maybe writing this way came most easily to him. Or he may have wanted to make it hard for anybody else to read the pages. Maybe he worried that other people might steal his ideas. Maybe he just wanted to keep his ideas secret.

Leonardo's interest in water went all the way back to his childhood, from the storms he saw. But water was only one of the subjects he planned to cover in his encyclopedia.

He wanted to understand and explain light— what was it made of? He wanted to understand how eyesight works, why birds can fly, and all the different parts of the human body. He came up with a list of about twenty big subjects. Just one page of a notebook might have little drawings of bird wings and feathers, along with thoughts about music and ideas for new weapons or sketches on

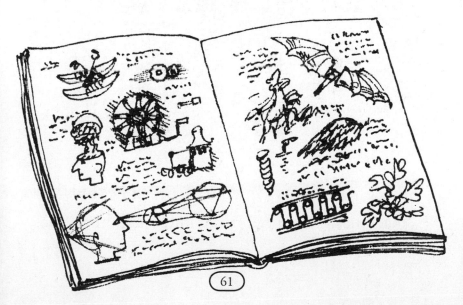

building dams. Leonardo never stuck to one subject. He'd go back and forth among many. The notebook pages are crammed with writing and beautiful drawings. It is almost as if whatever jumped into his mind, he put down on the page. What the notebooks reveal is the mind of a true genius.

Leonardo was interested in all kinds of machines. Machine parts interested him, too.

Screws and hinges and joints and hooks and springs. It may be strange to think of

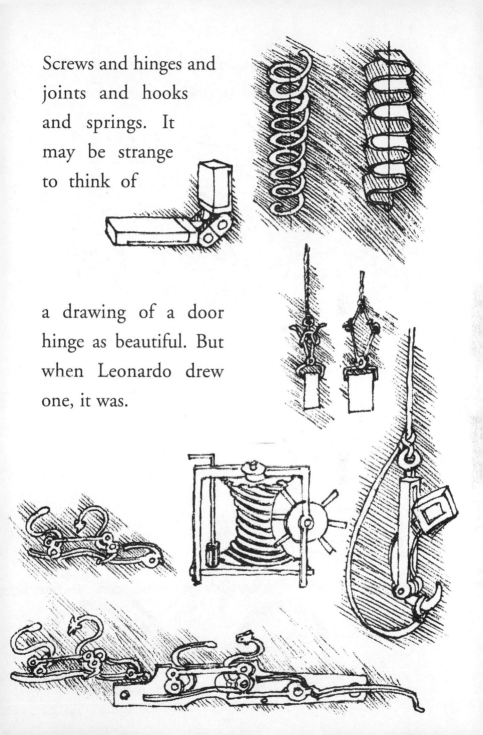

a drawing of a door hinge as beautiful. But when Leonardo drew one, it was.

He wanted to invent vehicles for people to use on land, in the air, even underwater.

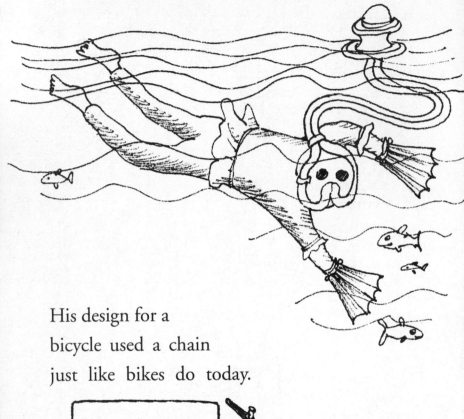

His design for a
bicycle used a chain
just like bikes do today.

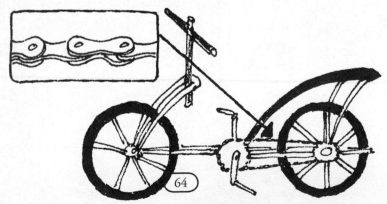

He designed a parachute
and something like
a submarine.

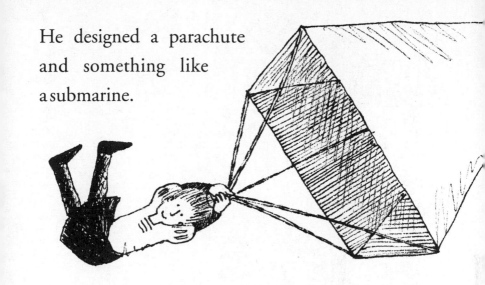

One of his notebook
drawings shows a
flying machine
with a rotor
blade at the top.
It was meant to twirl
around and around.
Like a helicopter.

Leonardo was sure that one day people would fly. He said, "It lies within the power of man to make this instrument." The story is that Leonardo would go to the marketplace, where he would buy birds in cages. Then he'd bring them home and set them free. How did they flap their wings? What made them able to fly? Why were they able to land safely without breaking their legs? He longed to discover the answers.

He made lots of drawings of bird wings. And how feathers grew on wings. He studied bats, too. And he made drawings of their wings. He tried to make wings for people that worked by using pulleys, cranks, wheels, and shock absorbers. One drawing had a pair of back pedals and a hand crank to make the wings move. Using another pair, a person would have had to flap the wings using muscle power. The wings' "bones" would be made of wood, the "muscles" from leather, and the "skin" from cloth.

Did Leonardo actually build any wings? Did anyone try them out? Nobody is sure. In the notebooks, he mentions testing the wings on a hill near Florence. If so, he may have jumped from the top of the hill and glided in the air for a little while. But he could not have flown. The wings would not have worked, for more than one reason. First, they were way too heavy. Also, it takes a lot of force to lift a heavy object off the ground and keep it in the air. The force of human power wasn't strong enough. And in Leonardo's day, engines with strong power had not yet been invented.

Of course, Leonardo was
right. People did learn to make flying
machines. But it didn't happen until December
of 1903. That is when the Wright brothers'
airplane flew for twelve seconds. That was almost
four hundred years after Leonardo died. He was a
man way ahead of his time.

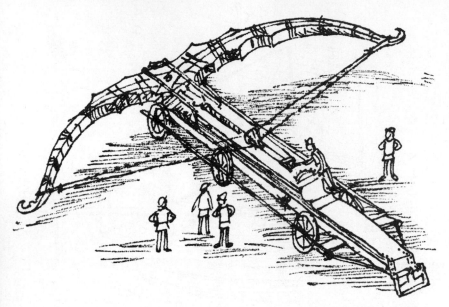

For a while, Leonardo worked for another duke in Italy. His name was Cesare Borgia. He was power-hungry and bloodthirsty. Leonardo designed weapons for the duke's troops to use in battle. Leonardo did not believe in war and referred to it as a disease.

But he did enjoy designing new and better war machinery. Some of the weapons look like something you'd see in a fantasy movie. There is one of a giant-size crossbow. It could shoot several arrows at one time. It was so big that several soldiers would have had to operate it. He also designed a strange contraption with long blades jutting out from it. It was supposed to strap onto a horse. The rider could attack his enemies, who couldn't get close enough to hurt him.

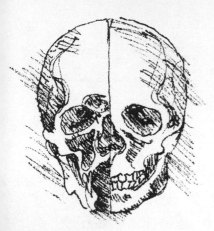
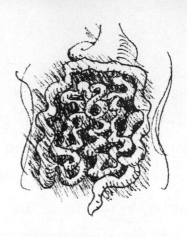

Leonardo thought of the human body as a machine, too. In fact, he considered it the most perfect machine. Leonardo wanted to understand the human body in the same way he came to understand horses: inside and out. He wanted to figure out how all the different parts of the body worked together. The best way to do this was to dissect bodies. This means cutting into a dead body. Peeling back different layers reveals how the body is built.

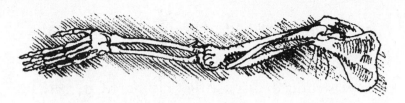

Today, medical students learn about the body by doing dissections. Sometimes doctors do dissections to understand why a person died. But Leonardo's time was very different. Medical students rarely ever did a dissection. They learned from books instead. The work of cutting into a dead body was considered too horrible.

Leonardo, however, was determined to see for himself. When he lived in Milan he had done some dissections of bodies. He wasn't a doctor or a medical student, so what he was doing was illegal. Later in his life he returned to Florence several times. There again he did more dissections. It is believed he worked on about thirty bodies. What he learned from them was put down in his notebooks. The drawings he did of the human body are astounding.

In Florence, he had a workshop in a hospital. He worked at night and he worked alone. The work was indeed disgusting. He hated it. But he did it, anyway.

The drawings were not discovered until long after Leonardo died. Nothing like them had ever been seen before. The drawings of a foot, for example, show it from three sides, moving in different ways. Leonardo also did cutaway drawings. He would draw a foot where one part had no skin. This was to let the muscles underneath show through.

He'd draw muscles to look like strings or ropes.

This was a good way to show which way a muscle pulled a limb. He'd also leave out some of the muscle to show the bones. With these drawings, there is no need for words. The drawings are better than words. They show everything exactly as it appears.

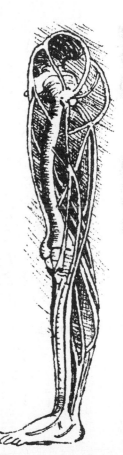

If the body was a machine, then it should be possible to build a mechanical man. In 1495, Leonardo made a design for the first robot. There

is some evidence that he built it, too. His robot was a full-size knight in armor that could sit up, move its head, and wave its arms. Again, Leonardo was hundreds of years ahead of his time.

Chapter 6
The Battle of the Artists

Leonardo   Michelangelo   Raphael

Leonardo was one the greatest artists of the Renaissance. But he was not alone. The Renaissance in Italy was such a special time because it produced so many talented artists. Besides Leonardo, the two other greatest names belong to Raphael and Michelangelo.

RAPHAEL

RAPHAEL SANZIO WAS BORN IN URBINO, ITALY, ON APRIL 6, 1483. HE FIRST LEARNED TO DRAW FROM HIS ARTIST FATHER. WHEN HE WAS TWENTY-ONE, HE WENT TO FLORENCE, WHERE HE STUDIED THE WORKS OF LEONARDO AND MICHELANGELO. IN HIS DAY, RAPHAEL WAS THE MOST POPULAR PAINTER. HIS LOVELY PICTURES OF MARY AND THE BABY JESUS HAVE A SPECIAL SWEETNESS AND HARMONY. HIS COLORS ARE STRONG AND PURE, NEVER JARRING. EVERYTHING IN A RAPHAEL PAINTING SEEMS TO BE EXACTLY WHERE IT BELONGS. LATER IN HIS CAREER, HE WORKED IN ROME FOR THE SAME POPE AS MICHELANGELO. RAPHAEL PAINTED TWO GIANT FRESCOES. ONE IS CALLED *THE SCHOOL OF ATHENS*, WHICH PORTRAYS THE GREAT THINKERS OF ANCIENT GREECE. PLATO AND ARISTOTLE STAND IN THE CENTER. SADLY, RAPHAEL DIED YOUNG, ON HIS THIRTY-SEVENTH BIRTHDAY.

MICHELANGELO

MICHELANGELO'S FULL NAME WAS
MICHELANGELO BUONARROTI. HE WAS
BORN IN CAPRESE, ITALY, IN 1475. HE
HAD A LONG AND SUCCESSFUL CAREER.
BUT HE DIDN'T CONSIDER PAINTING HIS
TRUE CALLING. HE THOUGHT OF HIMSELF
AS A SCULPTOR FIRST. HE LOVED
WORKING IN BEAUTIFUL ITALIAN MARBLE.
BESIDES HIS FAMOUS STATUE, *DAVID*,
IN FLORENCE, ANOTHER OF HIS GREAT
WORKS IS ONE OF MARY HOLDING
THE BODY OF JESUS. IT IS CALLED
THE PIETÀ AND WAS COMPLETED
WHEN HE WAS ONLY TWENTY-
THREE. *THE PIETÀ* IS FILLED
WITH A SAD TENDERNESS,
BUT MICHELANGELO IS
MAINLY KNOWN FOR
CREATING STRONG,
MUSCULAR FIGURES.

The
Pietà

FOR A SCULPTOR, HOWEVER, HE IS MOST
FAMOUS FOR PAINTING THE ENTIRE CEILING
OF A CHAPEL FOR THE POPE IN ROME:
THE CEILING OF THE SISTINE CHAPEL. IT
TOOK HIM FOUR YEARS, WORKING ON A
SCAFFOLD SIXTY FEET IN THE AIR. THE
FRESCO COVERS THE STORIES IN THE OLD
TESTAMENT STARTING WITH THE CREATION
OF THE WORLD.

Raphael was a great admirer of Leonardo's. Michelangelo was not. He didn't like Leonardo, and Leonardo didn't like him. It is hard to imagine two men who were more different. Michelangelo came from a well-off family but didn't wash or change his clothes often. He slept on the floor of his studio. He was also short, had a crooked back, and a quick temper. Leonardo was handsome, well-dressed, neatly groomed, and charming.

Twenty-three years younger than Leonardo, Michelangelo had become famous for his huge statue of David. Leonardo didn't think the statue was all that great. Or at least that's what he said.

In turn, Michelangelo made fun of Leonardo in public for never finishing his huge statue. He said, "You made a model of a horse you could never cast in bronze and which you gave up, to your shame. And the stupid people of Milan had faith in you!"

When both were asked to paint a wall in the main government building of Florence, it became a fierce contest. The walls were to picture different scenes from famous battles that Florence had won.

Again, the paintings were to be frescoes, pictures painted directly onto the walls. (The last time Leonardo had tried this was in the monastery for *The Last Supper*.) The room was giant-size, and

Leonardo's fresco was to measure about sixty feet by twenty-four feet. He began by making many drawings. He wanted a scene full of action, with horses rearing and soldiers fighting. The horror of war would come through, too: the dead. The wounded howling in pain. The dust and dirt and blood.

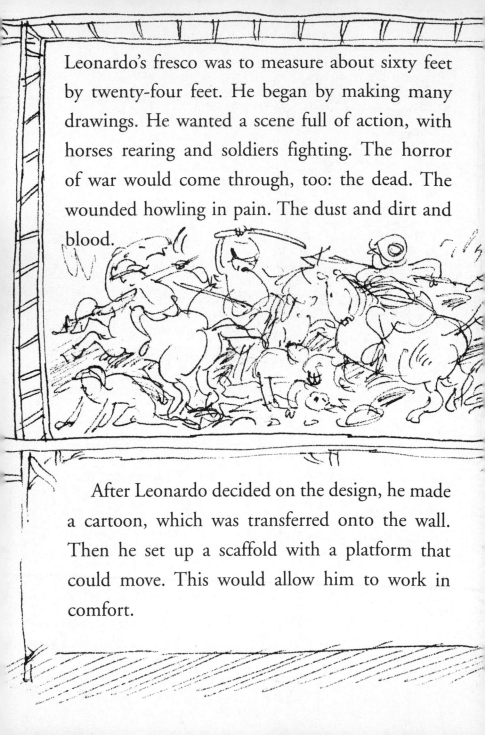

After Leonardo decided on the design, he made a cartoon, which was transferred onto the wall. Then he set up a scaffold with a platform that could move. This would allow him to work in comfort.

The trouble was, Leonardo still did not want to make a fresco in the usual way. Once again he tried an experiment. He found a way to use oil paints with coal fires to make the paint dry quickly. He

had tested out the experiment on a wall in his studio, and it had worked. But the test was done on a small paint-covered area. Leonardo needed it to work on great big areas—and it didn't. If the fires were placed close to the painting, it melted. If they were placed far away, there wasn't enough heat to make it dry. The top part of his battle scene ended up black with smoke; other parts ran. After three years of hard work, Leonardo was left with nothing but a great big mess.

As for Michelangelo, he didn't finish his wall, either. Maybe that was some comfort for Leonardo. In 1504, Michelangelo was called to Rome by the pope to start other jobs. One was to paint the ceiling of the pope's chapel. We know it as the Sistine Chapel.

CARTOONS OF THE 1500s

MODERN CARTOONS, WHICH ARE CREATED AS HUMOROUS COMIC STRIPS IN NEWSPAPERS AND MAGAZINES, ARE NOT THE SAME THING AS RENAISSANCE CARTOONS. A CARTOON WAS A DRAWING, ONE OF THE STEPS IN MAKING A FRESCO. THE ARTIST WOULD DRAW EVERYTHING TO SIZE, JUST AS IT WOULD APPEAR ON THE WALL. THE CARTOON WOULD BE FIXED TO THE WALL. THEN SMALL HOLES WERE PUNCHED ALL ALONG THE LINES OF THE DRAWING. AFTER

The drawing is put up on the wall.

Holes are punched along the lines.

THAT, THE ARTIST WOULD GO OVER THE LINES WITH CHARCOAL. WHEN THE CARTOON WAS TAKEN OFF THE WALL, AN OUTLINE IN CHARCOAL REMAINED. NOW THE ARTIST WAS READY TO START ON THE FULL-COLOR PAINTING. THE CARTOONS OF LEONARDO'S THAT STILL EXIST ARE BEAUTIFUL WORKS OF ART THEMSELVES. THE CARTOON FOR THE BATTLE SCENE WAS KEPT BY THE CITY OF FLORENCE. OFFICIALS FELT IT WAS OWED TO THEM AFTER LEONARDO RUINED THE WALL. TODAY IT IS IN A MUSEUM.

3.

Charcoal is rubbed over the lines.

4.

The cartoon is taken down, leaving the outline.

Chapter 7
Leonardo's Ladies

Not everything in Leonardo's career ended in failure. Sometimes he actually finished a job. It is true that only ten completed paintings are known to be by Leonardo. That's a tiny number. But each and every one is a treasure.

The story is that in 1505 a rich silk merchant wanted a portrait of his wife. He asked Leonardo to paint it. Leonardo had told friends that he had "grown weary of the paintbrush." He meant that painting didn't bring him much joy anymore. But perhaps he needed the money. Or perhaps the woman's face caught his interest, especially her smile. Whatever the reason, Leonardo took the job. And he finished the painting although he worked on it for many years.

Nobody knows for sure what the woman's name was. Her first name may have been Lisa. She may have been Lisa del Giocondo. In English, the painting is called the *Mona Lisa*.

In the portrait, only the top half of Mona Lisa's body is shown. Behind her is a landscape. A winding road leads back to craggy mountains that disappear in mist.

Mona Lisa's black dress is very simple. And she does not wear fancy jewelry. A thin black veil covers her long curling hair. Then, as now, it was the custom for widows to wear black. So perhaps Mona Lisa was not the wife of a silk merchant. Perhaps she was someone else about whom we know nothing. It is one of the mysteries surrounding the painting.

Her hands are crossed and rest one on top of the other. They are very graceful with soft, long fingers. Looking at them, it is easy to believe there is muscle and bone beneath the skin. It is possible to forget that her hands are just brushstrokes of paint on a flat surface.

But it is the expression on her face that draws people to her. Her lips are pressed together in a calm half-smile. She looks as if she is keeping a secret. Her eyes are full of mystery, too. They appear to look out at something only she can see.

At the Louvre

The *Mona Lisa* is probably the most famous painting in the world. Why? No one can really answer that question. But Leonardo loved the painting, too. When he was finished, he decided to keep it. In fact, he kept it with him, wherever he went, for the rest of his life.

Many people consider another portrait of a woman by Leonardo even more beautiful than the *Mona Lisa*. It is all called *Young Girl with Ermine*. An ermine is a type of weasel. In winter, its coat turns white—just as it appears in the painting. Ermine hairs were used for paintbrushes. So it's possible that Leonardo painted the ermine with an ermine brush!

Why is an ermine in the picture? It may be there as a play on words. The young girl's name was Cecilia Gallerani. And *gale* in Greek means "ermine."

As in the *Mona Lisa*, only the top half of the young girl is painted. But there is no landscape behind her. She stands against a dark solid background. Neither she nor the animal looks directly at the viewer. Instead, her face is turned so that she is gazing off to the side. At what or at whom? No one knows. She wears richer clothes than the Mona Lisa's. A long strand of beads is looped around her neck. Her dress is part blue, part red, with gold lining and black trim. The fabric looks as if it is made of velvet.

Mona Lisa is dreamy looking. The young lady here looks like she has a quick, sharp mind. You can see it in her alert eyes, the set of her mouth and chin. One hand holds the ermine closely against her shoulder. The ermine looks alert and

intelligent, too. The girl's hand is beautiful. It's painted to perfection. But her thin fingers are tense. Mona Lisa's fingers are plump and relaxed. Through the poses and the faces, Leonardo catches the soul of two very different women.

Young Girl with Ermine is not as famous as the *Mona Lisa*. It hangs in a museum in Kraków, Poland. The *Mona Lisa* is in the Louvre, a famous museum in Paris where crowds come every day to see her. Which painting is more beautiful? People lucky enough to see both must decide that for themselves.

Another Leonardo portrait of a young woman is in the National Gallery of Art in Washington, D.C. It is the only painting by Leonardo in the United States. Her name was Ginevra de' Benci. It is even smaller than the *Mona Lisa* or *Young Girl with Ermine*. The bottom was cut off at some point, so now the painting shows only Ginevra's head and chest. Her skin is almost ghostly pale.

Ginevra de' Benci, c. 1474

Her eyes seem sorrowful. It is very hard to "read" her expression. That is one of the reasons why people keep looking at the painting. *Portrait of Ginevra de' Benci* is haunting.

Chapter 8
Losses

In 1504, Leonardo's father, Ser Piero, died. He was seventy-eight years old. There was no will, and Leonardo ended up receiving nothing. All the money went to Ser Piero's other children.

Then, in 1507, Leonardo's uncle Francesco died. He had been the only relative to show him any affection. Francesco did have a will. Everything was left to Leonardo. Francesco wanted Leonardo to have all his land and money. But Leonardo's half brothers and sisters were furious. They went to court. What Leonardo ended up getting was the *use* of Francesco's land and money. After Leonardo died, it would all go to his relatives.

Leonardo was almost sixty. He had health problems. He had no home and not all that much to show for his many years of work. But at a time when he needed a patron, one appeared. The man appreciated Leonardo for the genius he was. He provided him with a lovely home and garden. He let Leonardo bring along Salai and his other good friend, Francesco Melzi. All the man asked of Leonardo was his company.

The man also happened to be a king.

King Francis I of France had a grand house in Amboise. That's in the northern part of France. Leonardo was given a beautiful brick-and-limestone house to live in. He brought along his book collection, his notebooks, and three of his paintings. One of them was the *Mona Lisa*.

A tunnel connected the two houses. Each day he was in Amboise, the king would come to visit and talk. He would pick a subject and ask Leonardo his opinions. The king evidently felt it was an honor simply to be in Leonardo's presence.

And so Leonardo finished out his life in France. On May 2, 1519, he died. One story says that he died in the king's arms. Another says that his last words were about his horse statue. If only he had been able to complete it.

He was buried in a chapel in Amboise. It may not be a happy ending. But it isn't a sad one, either.

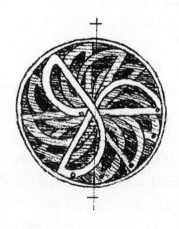

THE NOTEBOOKS

LEONARDO LEFT HIS NOTEBOOKS TO HIS FRIEND MELZI, WHO TRIED TO ORGANIZE THEM. ALL THE PAGES ON ART WERE ASSEMBLED AND PUBLISHED AS A BOOK. IT WAS CALLED *TREATISE ON PAINTING*. A TREATISE EXPLAINS A PERSON'S IDEAS ON A SUBJECT. SO THIS BOOK EXPLAINS LEONARDO'S IDEAS ABOUT PAINTING. FOR SOME REASON, THE BOOK WASN'T PUBLISHED UNTIL 1651, MORE THAN 130 YEARS AFTER LEONARDO'S DEATH.

THE REST OF THE NOTEBOOK PAGES REMAINED UNKNOWN TO THE WORLD FOR FAR LONGER. THE SHEETS THAT WEREN'T LOST OR STOLEN OR CUT APART DIDN'T COME TO LIGHT UNTIL THE EARLY 1800S. THE MOST RECENT ONES WERE FOUND IN 1965. THEY TURNED UP IN MADRID, IN THE STACKS OF THE NATIONAL LIBRARY!

Leonardo

Leonardo

TIMELINE OF LEONARDO DA VINCI'S LIFE

1452 — 1452 Leonardo is born on April 15

1468 — Leonardo becomes an apprentice in Verrocchio's studio in Florence

1473 — Leonardo becomes a member of the painters' guild

1476 — Leonardo's *Annunciation*

1478 — Leonardo's *Portrait of Ginevra de' Benci*

1482 — Leonardo leaves Florence to work in Milan; around this time he begins keeping notebooks

1490 — Leonardo is working on his horse statue

1490 — *The Feast of Paradise* is put on for the wedding feast of the duke's nephew; Salai comes to live with Leonardo

1493 — Leonardo's *Young Girl with Ermine*

1495 — Leonardo may have tried out one of his flying machines

1498 — Approximately when Leonardo finishes the fresco for *The Last Supper* outside Milan

1499 — The French army attacks Milan and destroys the model of the horse statue

1499–1500 — Leonardo leaves Milan

1502 — Leonardo works for Cesare Borgia

1503 — Leonardo is back in Florence; approximately when Leonardo begins painting *Mona Lisa*

1506 — Leonardo gives up on the battle scene fresco in Florence's town hall

1506 — Leonardo returns to Milan, where he remains, on and off, for many years

1516 — Leonardo moves to Amboise as the guest of the king of France

1519 — Leonardo dies on May 2

TIMELINE OF THE WORLD

Johannes Gutenberg devises movable-type printing press — **1450s**

Nicolaus Copernicus, the Polish astronomer, is born — **1473**

Michelangelo Buonarroti is born — **1475**

Bartholomeu Dias of Portugal rounds the southern tip of Africa — **1488**

Christopher Columbus sails to the New World — **1492**

Süleyman I, later emperor of the Ottoman Empire, is born — **1494**

Vasco da Gama finds a sea route to India — **1497–99**

Michelangelo's statue of David; young Raphael comes to Florence to study with Leonardo and Michelangelo — **1504**

The architect Donato Bramante is hired by the pope to rebuild St. Peter's church in Rome — **1506**

Leonardo's friend, the explorer Amerigo Vespucci, publishes his account of sailing to the New World; the New World is named America after Vespucci — **1507**

Michelangelo finishes painting the Sistine Chapel; Gerardus Mercator, who produces the first map of the world, is born — **1512**

Andreas Vesalius, who publishes the first accurate book on human anatomy, is born in Brussels — **1514**

Ferdinand Magellan begins the first voyage around the world — **1519**

Queen Elizabeth I is born — **1533**

BIBLIOGRAPHY

Bramly, Serge. **Leonardo: The Artist and the Man.** Penguin Books, New York, 1994.

Byrd, Robert. **Leonardo, Beautiful Dreamer.** Dutton Children's Books, New York, 2003.

Canaday, John. **What Is Art? An Introduction to Painting, Sculpture, and Architecture.** Alfred A. Knopf, New York, 1980.

Fritz, Jean. **Leonardo's Horse.** G. P. Putnam's Sons, New York, 2001.

Galluzzi, Paolo. **Mechanical Marvels: Invention in the Age of Leonardo.** Giunti, Florence. 1996.

Langley, Andrew. **Eyewitness: Leonardo & His Times.** DK Publishing Inc., New York, 2000.

McLanathan, Richard B.K. **Leonardo da Vinci.** Harry N. Abrams, Inc., Publishers, New York, 1990.

Stanley, Diane. **Leonardo da Vinci.** Morrow Junior Books, New York, 1996.

Ventura, Piero. **Great Painters.** G. P. Putnam's Sons, New York, 1984.